PLUSH FRIENDS

PLUSH FRIENDS

Reflections in the time of COVID-19

Emilia Kate Zados

Published by Tablo

Dedication

We all had that one plush toy that is forever in our hearts.

This book is dedicated to my big brother Henry, who at 38 Passed from a Malignant Brain Tumor holding his childhood toy Scally the Mouse.

Preface

The COVID-19 Pandemic that hit the world in 2019/2020 will be remembered as a catastrophic event that changed the world as we know it. As I publish this book, I am all to aware that a second, more deadly wave of this virus could face us at any moment, and that the real impact of this deadly virus on human lives and the economy is yet to be known and likely immeasurable.

The way we each experience life will continue to shift as we cautiously attempt to find our feet - a "new normal". With our memories scarred by images from media outlets across the world, we, as Australian's can acknowledge that we have been truly lucky. While unemployment and loneliness hit us hard throughout this tough time, our Nation has fought against this deadly virus, committing to several weeks without our usual routines and social networks. This has hurt us. For many, it will be the most unsettling period of our lives. We have lost lives, jobs, businesses, relationships, freedom and morale. But we have not lost our sense of community, nor our desire to make the best out of an uncomfortable situation. We are resilient.

When I found myself unemployed for the first time in early April 2020 with no gym, no social outlets and no hectic schedule to fill my days, I turned to walking for hours on end throughout the suburban streets to pass my time. While at first, I saw every human walking or jogging within ten feet of me as a biological hazard, I soon began to open my eyes and see the wonderful acts of humanity taking part during such a difficult time. Then I began to notice a sense of playfulness in the things people were doing to keep busy and entertained. At first, I saw a couple of furry plush toys on the fences of local homes poking out from behind multicoloured chalk drawings on footpaths and walls. Then up popped the drawings of rainbows in front windows in acknowledgement of our frontline healthcare workers.

As the plush toys began to multiply in mass, I began to notice hand-written signs indicating that a 'Bear Hunt' was taking place. The more I looked, the more I spotted little furry faces in windows, poking out of letterboxes, mounted on garden stakes and sitting on patio seats as though watching the passers-by. And I become addicted, at first snapping away with my i-phone and sharing the photos with my significant other and then realising the real impact of having something playful to take part in - a sense of community and a reason to smile.

I created this book, 'Plush Friends' as a gesture to the tough period that we refer to as 'COVID-19'. While in Australia, we have not experienced the deadliness of Coronavirus on the same scale as other continents, we will undoubtedly remember 2020 as one of the most unusual and difficult years. In five, ten or fifteen years time, I believe we will look back at this time and reflect on the uniqueness of it, remembering how we embraced it by becoming more creative, more playful and more community-minded.

In 2020, we got to know our neighbours. We stayed home, we cooked more, we talked on the phone more, we pulled out the puzzles and board games and we walked, walked and walked. And on our walks, we were joined by many plush friends, who from the safety of their homes, candidly reminded us that we are not, and will never be alone - and there is always a reason to smile.

x Millie Kate

Acknowledgements

I would like to thank all that took the time to answer the 'plush friends' questionnaire that was essential for me to create this book. I appreciate the effort and heartfelt responses by all.

A special mention to Jan Reid from Elsternwick who changed up her 'Menagerie' of plush toys weekly to keep the locals smiling and to the Rovay Gallery in Middle Park, who have offered to donate 30% of profits to the Save The Children Foundation COVID-19 Crisis Appeal upon mention of this book.

Finally, a heartfelt thank you to my partner, Anton, who encouraged me with this project from day one. I couldn't have done this without your support and tough love.

"

Amidst the challenges of COVID-19, we have created space to slow down, to observe our lives, and appreciate the greatness that the smaller things bring.

We're All Going On A...

*No Plush Friends were hurt during the making of this publication!

'Happypotamus', Elsternwick

HAPPYPOTAMUS

I Belong To: *Tony , Elsternwick*

Why did you decide to put Happypotamus on your fence?
I didn't decide; he just appeared one day! They're very territorial you know and it's a jungle out there!

Favorite 'Stay at Home' activity:
Netflix, tidying up, building projects and reading.

Best Advice:

"

All clouds eventually drift away and the sunshine returns.

What positive habit will you hang onto once restrictions ease:
An holistic appreciation of toilet paper. Quantity is equally as important as quality!

'Anonymous Lamb', Elsternwick

ANONYMOUS LAMB

I Belong To: *Anonymous, Elsternwick*
Anonymous Lamb lives alongside Happypottamus in Elsternwick. He turned up on the adjacent fence to Happypotumus during the early stages of the COVID-19 pandemic. The two are fondly known by locals as the trend-starters of the street with bears and plush toys turning up in many of the neighboring homes following these two friends.

Favorite 'Stay At Home' activity during the COVID-19 crisis?
Dog Watching! We love taking daily walks to the park to meet and observe all the wonderfully different dogs of all sizes and personalities!

Best Advice:

❝

Even when it's raining, keep moving.

What Positive Habits will you hang onto once restrictions ease
Daily Meditation is a must for the soul and create every meal with love.

'Gertie & Pup', St Kilda West

GERTIE & PUP

We Belong To: *The Knight Family, St Kilda West*

❝

We Love less traffic, less deadlines and the slower pace.

Why did you decide to take part in the 'Bear Hunt?'
To share a bit of happiness and joy for children- and we love dogs!

Favourite Stay At Home Activity during the COVID-19 Crisis?
Taking our real dogs to the park and not having to rush back.

Best Advice:
Try and find some joy , such as taking time to notice the leaves changing colour.

What Positive Habit will you hang onto once restrictions ease?
Continue to appreciate the small things that nature brings!

'Ted', Brighton

TED

I Belong To: *Maximus, Brighton*

" "

"Stay strong, stay positive and try to get outside at least once a day for a walk"

Why did you decide to take part in the 'Bear Hunt?'
I saw a post on Facebook about children doing this for other children to help them connect and have something to do while on daily exercise. I thought it was a great idea and immediately wanted to take part.

Favorite 'Stay At Home' activity:
Being pushed fast up and down the hallway on my ride on motorbike!

What Positive Habit will you hang onto once restrictions ease? *Daily walks!*

'Bomber, Harry & Eyore', Doreen

BOMBER, HARRY & EYORE

We Belong To: *Steph .P. , Doreen*

"

It was so important to not confuse physical distancing and 'social' distancing.

Why did you decide to take part in the 'Bear Hunt?'
With the current state of the world I just wanted to be apart of something that could bring some joy to people while walking down the street.

Favourite Stay At Home Activity during the COVID-19 Crisis?
Turning our new house into a family home.

Best Advice?
Try to have your down time space outside of the rooms you spend every day in. It's important to still give yourself time to disconnect and wind down.

What Positive Habit will you hang onto when restrictions are lifted?
Going for a thirty minute walk every day. The little bit of fresh air really helps lift my spirits. This time has also taught me how imperative it is to touch base with people you may not normally reach out to that you usually see in person.

'Lucky' (in love), Elwood

LUCKY (IN LOVE)

I Belong To: *Anonymous, Elwood*

Why did you decide to take part in the 'Bear Hunt?'
I found this cute little bear on the ground when I was walking with my dog. I figured he must've belonged to someone special, so I called him 'Lucky' and stuck him in the gate in hope that he would find his home. He made me smile.

Favourite Stay At Home Activity during the COVID-19 Crisis?
I have loved embracing my 'inner child' during this time. I have been painting, drawing and dancing the way I remember as a child.

Best Advice?

"

Do you! After all of this, you will have a better 'you' to present to the world!

What Positive Habit will you hang onto once restrictions ease?
Being more creative, whether it be with my free time, my thoughts or my actions, I am dedicated to creativity.

'Teddy Says', Rovay Gallery Middle Park

TEDDY SAYS

I Belong To: *Rovay Walk-By Window Gallery, Middle Park*

The Rovay Walk-By Window Gallery is located at 310 Richardson Street, Middle Park. The Gallary owners, who pride themselves on their dedication to the community have kindly offered to donate 30% of artwork sales price to the **Save The Children Foundation COVID-19 Crisis Appeal** *if mentioned at the time of purchase.*

Why did you decide to take part in the 'Bear Hunt?'
To inspire passing by children to get involved with the art via the "teddy says" thought bubble.

Favourite Stay At Home Activity during the COVID-19 Crisis?
Creating and Exhibiting Art

Best Advice?

"

Creativity is Contagious. Pass it on- Albert Einstein

What Positive Habit will you hang onto when restrictions are lifted?
Maintaining regular monthly art exhibitions to cheer and contribute to people's well being.

'Pinky & Pedro', Glenroy

PINKY & PEDRO

We Belong To: *Bec and Arden*

Why did you decide to take part in the 'Bear Hunt?'
To bring smiles to others faces, especially the younger ones who don't fully comprehend why they can't go out and play with their friends.

Favourite Stay At Home Activity during the COVID-19 Crisis?
Using our sourdough starter to bake bread and experiment with other things such as crumpets, pita bread and pancakes.

Best Advice?
Remember to take a breath and some time for yourself but also that there is support available out there, whether financial, medical or mental health services.

"

Don't be afraid to reach out, even just for a chat.

What Positive Habit will you hang once restrictions ease?
Morning meditation and journaling before rushing to our computers to start work. This helps to reduce over working but also to reflect on the previous day.

'Lulu The Lemur', Elsternwick

LULU THE LEMUR

I Belong To: *Olive .P. , Elsternwick*

Why did you decide to take part in the 'Bear Hunt?'
I decided to put my plush friend out because i wanted other kids to do the same.

Favourite 'Stay At Home' activity during the COVID-19 Crisis? *Going for bike rides, playing board games and cooking.*

Best Advice?

"

Enjoy the Little things in life that are free light sunsets and the beach!

What Positive Habit will you hang onto once restrictions ease?
Doing more walks and spending more time with family and friends.

'Melon, Sia, Bonniem Fluffy, Sam & Cutie', Elsternwick

MELON, SIA, BONNIE, FLUFFY, SAM & CUTIE

We Belong To: *Libby .W. , Elsternwick*

Why did you decide to take part in the 'Bear Hunt?'
Because through this time, people are kinda sad and i wanted to cheer them up.

Favourite 'Stay At Home Activity' during the COVID-19 Crisis?
Sewing or Knitting.

Best Advice?

"

Work out a plan that suits you!

What Positive Habit will you hang onto once restrictions ease?
Remembering that we are lucky to have our families.

'Pinky', Elsternwick

PINKY

I Belong To: *Ava, Elsternwick*

Why did you decide to take part in the 'Bear Hunt?'
Because of 'COVID-19'...

❝

It was a nice thing for the children to spot the bears when going for a walk.

Favourite Stay At Home Activity during the COVID-19 Crisis?
Playing Monopoly!

Best Advice?
Stay positive. Appreciate these quiet times and the good things that come with it.

What Positive Habit will you hang onto once restrictions ease?
Going for long walks along the beach.

'Bunny, Monkey, Bear & Friends', Elsternwick

BUNNY, MONKEY & BEAR

We Belong To: *Johnny .R. , Elsternwick*

Why did you decide to take part in the 'Bear Hunt?'
We did this when we saw others staying at home doing this. (Community!)

Favourite Stay At Home Activity during the COVID-19 Crisis?
Watching movies, Playing Ping Pong and Cuddling the Cat.

Best Advice:

"

Stay @ Home!

What Positive Habit will you hang onto once restrictions ease?
Being more grateful.

'Kozi, Love & Friendship', Elsternwick

KOZI, LOVE & FRIENDSHIP

We Belong To: *Laws/Horton Family, Elsternwick*

"

Treat everybody with respect and assist people who need it. People have got to know their neighbours!

Why did you decide to take part in the 'Bear Hunt?'
To brighten up the day for all that walk past!

Favourite Stay At Home Activity during the COVID-19 Crisis?
Reading & Cooking.

Best Advice?
Stay Strong and Ask for Help if needed!

What Positive Habit will you hang onto once restrictions ease?
More time with the family and getting to know the neighbours.

'Ted & Frog' Reading 'Grug' in the window, Elsternwick

TED & FROG

We Belong To: *Quade, who lives in Rural NSW and is missed dearly by his grandmother!*

"

The Bear Hunt is a great community activity and of course it's great to make the children and adults smile.

Favourite 'Stay At Home' Activity during the COVID-19 Crisis
Jigsaw Puzzles!

Best Advice:?
We will get through this.

What Positive Habit will you hang onto once restrictions ease?
More time with the family and getting to know the neighbours.

'The Menagerie', Weeks 1-3, Gardenvale

'The Menagerie', Weeks 4-6, Gardenvale

"THE MENAGERIE"

We Belong To: *Jan .R. , Gardenvale*

Each week on a Tuesday, Jan changed up her 'Menagerie' to keep her contribution lively, relevant and exciting for the local community. From Easter eggs to Autumn leaves to birds flying over the rainbow from the 'Wizard of Oz', Jan's Managerie has been a particularly special contribution to the 'Bear Hunt'.

Why did you decide to take part in the 'Bear Hunt?'
It's been such a difficult time and i wanted to give cheer to people walking past and give them a focus and a smile.

Favorite 'Stay At Home' Activity:
Painting! I've locked myself in the studio during this time.

Best Advice?

"

Look for the magic in the day. It may just be the sunshine, a flower in your garden or a message from a friend.

What Positive Habit will you hang onto once restrictions ease?
Working in the studio!

"Big Ted", Middle Park

BIG TED

I Belong To: *James, aged 13 , Middle Park*

Big Ted is Frequently found next door with 'Little Ted', where he keeps the seat warm and has a better view of passers-by.

Why did you decide to take part in the 'Bear Hunt?'
James' favourite book when he was younger was "we're going on a bear hunt" and he thought young kids might like to pretend they are on a bear hunt while out walking during COVID-19.

Favourite 'Stay At Home' Activity during the COVID-19 Crisis?
Playing too much online Gaming with friends.

"

You have each other, and your health, which is priceless.

What Positive habit will you hang onto when restrictions are lifted?
Home cooking and creating new recipes.

'Little Ted', Middle Park

LITTLE TED

I Belong To: *Leo, 3 years old, Middle Park*

Why did you decide to take part in the 'Bear Hunt?'
Our neighbours had 'Big Ted' and we wanted to encourage others to get out and spot the teddy's.

Favourite 'Stay At Home' Activity during the COVID-19 Crisis?
Lots of gardening and playing in the mud!

Best Advice?

" "

Listen to lots of lovely music that makes you happy. We recommend 'Mary Poppins'- we've watched it so many times.

What Positive Habit will you hang onto once restrictions ease?
Spending more time outside, going for more walks and staying in contact with neighbours.

'Rainbows & Kisses', Elsternwick

RAINBOWS & KISSES

I Belong To: '*The Adler Clan*'

❝

Stay safe everybody! We are in this together and will get through tough times with good times ahead. Light is at the end of the tunnel.

Why did you decide to take part in the 'Bear Hunt?'
A butterfly is always a happy sight; colourful and bright for everyone to enjoy.

Favorite 'Stay At Home' Activity:
Dancing to the various genres of music being played by my parents and siblings, playing our old board games together that we played when we were younger.

Best Advice?
There are people who are willing to support you. Reach out to them as that's what they are there for.

What positive habit will you hang onto once restrictions ease?
Spending more quality time together as a family and continuing to play games together.

'Timmy', Elwood

"TIMMY"

I Belong To: *Emilia Kate, Elwood*

Timmy is a special feature as he belongs to the author! I've had Timmy since I was two years old. He has been through a lot with me and has lost most, if not all of his appendages at some stage!

"

I believe age is only a number. Timmy still sits proudly on my bed!

Why did you decide to take part in the 'Bear Hunt?'
I've always had a place in my heart for my childhood toy, Timmy the leopard. Naturally, I have a great appreciation for all of these wonderfully unique plush friends that bring us comfort during the tough times.

Favourite Stay At Home Activity during the COVID-19 Crisis?
Spotting and taking photos of plush toys on my walks, of course! I also started working on a mosaic, which takes a lot of patience!

Best Advice:
Think about how and where you spend your money. I am so mindful of supporting small businesses and local farms. I make a conscious effort to buy the independent brands. I love knowing I am supporting the local community.

What Positive Habit will you hang onto once restrictions ease?
I have learnt to not be so strict with myself. It's completely ok to just go for a walk and skip the gym. Naps are also okay and Sunday's can be spent just reading, walking and cooking!

Afterword

Producing 'Plush Friends' has been a humbling journey that has really taught me that it's the 'small things' in life that matter. Thank you from the bottom of my heart for taking the time to purchase and read this book. While there were hundreds of cute, funny and unique 'plush friends' that I would have liked to have starred in this publication, this is a brief snapshot that represents many of our journeys through the challenging 'COVID-19' isolation period.

A percentage of the profits of this book will be donated to the **Save The Children Foundation COVID-19 Crisis Appeal**. By Purchasing this book, you have helped children in need that have been deeply affected survive this pandemic.

For more information, visit savethechildren.org.au

Keep walking, stay safe and remember that your neighbours are only a stone throw away!

About The Author

Born in Melbourne and residing in the leafy Bayside suburbs for most of her adult life, Emilia Kate Zados aka "Millie" is a Project Manager by day and a writer by night. Usually writing for her personal opinion blog or scribbling away in her journal, Millie sees writing as a special way of reflecting on her thoughts and ideas and a place to put her imagination to work.

Among other qualifications, Millie Majored in Jouralism at Monash University, before later deciding to study a Post Graduate qualification in Project Management to pursue this career path instead.

Millie has always been passionate about books and writing. Much of her childhood was spent basking in the literary delights of Enid Blyton, R.L. Stine Bryce Courtenay. Her style is varied - from blog style to poetry, to this playful and heartfelt gift that you hold in your hands, 'Plush Friends.'

Millie loves the challenges that writing brings. She is currently undertaking William Whitecloud's course 'Writers Genius' and takes much of her inspiration from him. In the midst of the COVID 'lock-down', and on her regular meanderings through the winding streets, she has been inspired by your 'Plush Friends' and reminds us the importance of embracing our softer side.